THIS WALKER BOOK BELONGS TO:

_____

_____

_____

_____

For Carol and Peter

First published 1998 by Walker Books Ltd
87 Vauxhall Walk, London SE11 5HJ

This edition published 2003

2 4 6 8 10 9 7 5 3

© 1998, 2003 Paul Dowling

The right of Paul Dowling to be identified as author/illustrator
of this work has been asserted by him in accordance with
the Copyright, Designs and Patents Act 1988

This book has been typeset in Gill Sans Schoolbook

Printed in China

British Library Cataloguing in Publication Data:
a catalogue record for this book
is available from the British Library

ISBN 0-7445-9836-2

www.walkerbooks.co.uk

Beans on Toast
The Story of Baked Beans

Paul Dowling

WALKER BOOKS
AND SUBSIDIARIES
LONDON · BOSTON · SYDNEY · AUCKLAND

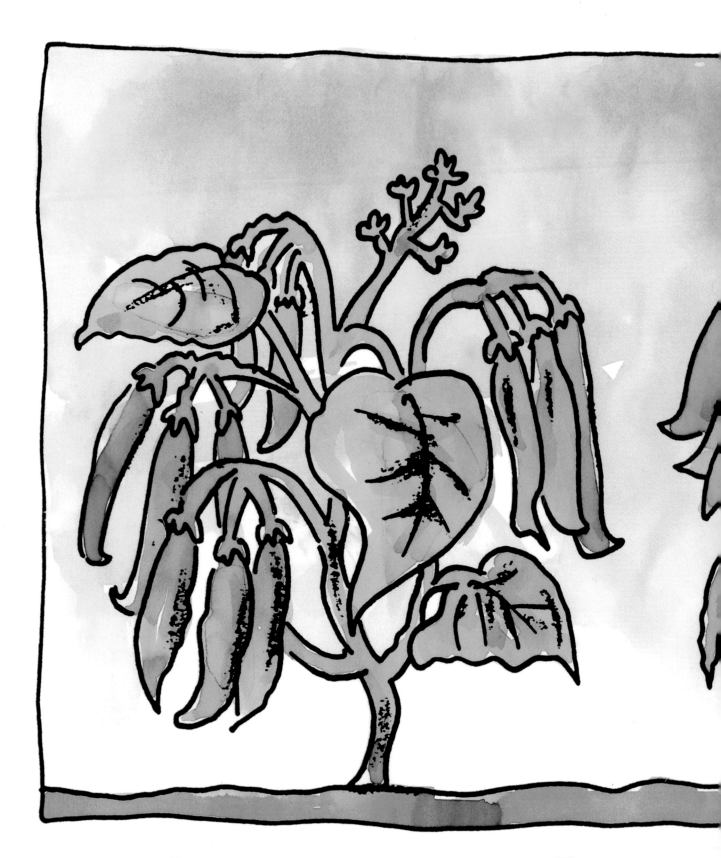

Beans on stalks

Beans on legs

Beans on racks

Beans on wheels

Beans on the road

Beans on cranes

Beans on the boil

Beans on tins

Beans on trucks

Beans on shelves

Beans on the counter

Beans on the way home

Beans on cooker

Beans on spoon

Beans on head

Beans on floor

Beans on toast

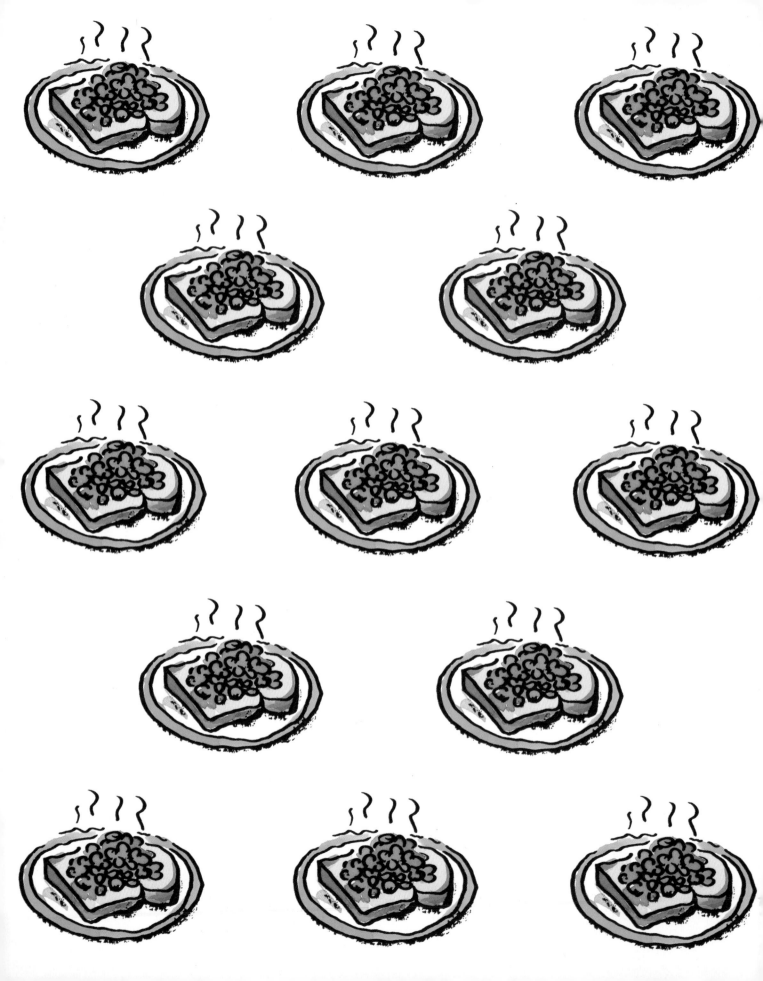